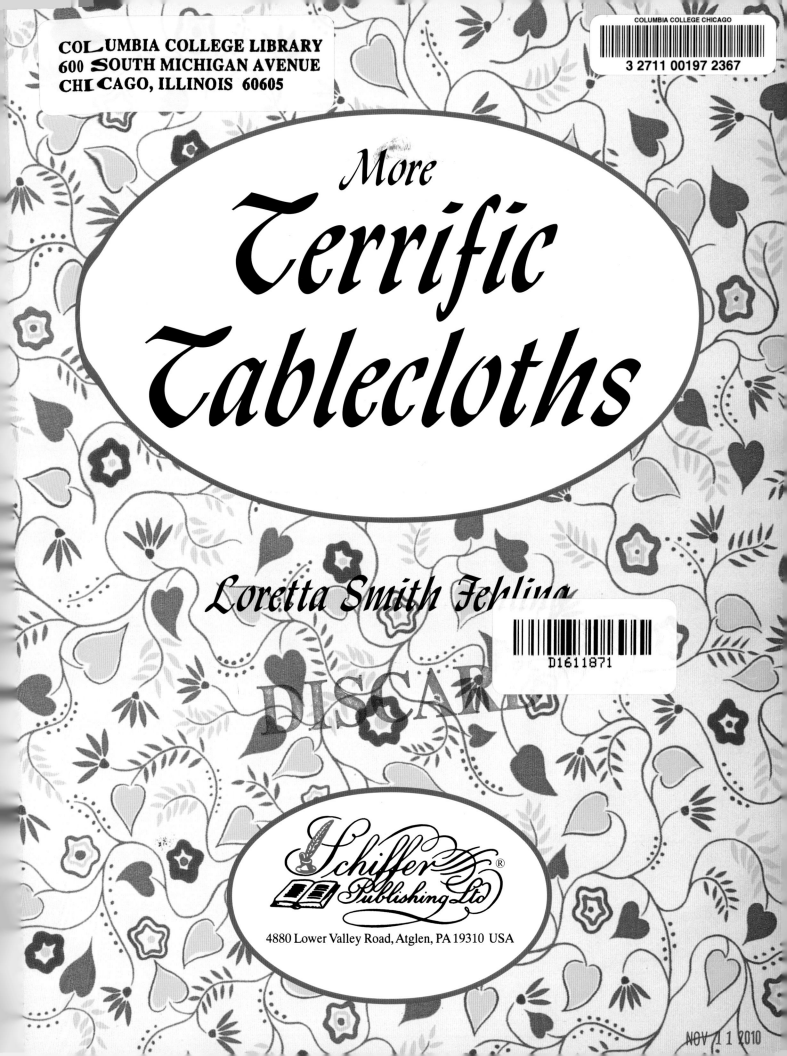

# *More* Terrific Tablecloths

*Loretta Smith Fehling*

Schiffer Publishing Ltd

4880 Lower Valley Road, Atglen, PA 19310 USA

# Dedication

To my mother, Priscilla Smith, who instilled in me, at a very early age, a love for sewing and all textiles.

# Acknowledgments

Thanks to all the people who recognize that table-cloths are worth saving and using. A special thanks to all of my patrons who have purchased my clothing. They allow me to make my living in a very special way and to continue my search for beautiful tablecloths.

Copyright © 1999 by Loretta Smith Fehling
Library of Congress Catalog Card Number: 99-63914

Book Layout by Anne Davidsen
Type set in Lydian Cursive/Korinna

ISBN: 0-7643-0975-7

Printed in China
1 2 3 4

Published by Schiffer Publishing Ltd.
4880 Lower Valley Road
Atglen, PA 19310
Phone: (610) 593-1777;
Fax: (610) 593-2002
E-mail: Schifferbk@aol.com
Please visit our web site catalog at
**www.schifferbooks.com**

This book may be purchased from the publisher.
Include $3.95 for shipping.
Please try your bookstore first.
We are interested in hearing from authors
with book ideas on related subjects.
You may write for a free catalog.

In Europe, Schiffer books are distributed by
Bushwood Books
6 Marksbury Rd.
Kew Gardens
Surrey TW9 4JF England
Phone: 44 (0)181 392-8585;
Fax: 44 (0)181 392-9876
E-mail: Bushwd@aol.com

# Contents

# Introduction

This companion volume to *Terrific Tablecloths* amazes me. The first volume had over 400 tablecloth designs and this one includes almost 300. When I first started collecting tablecloths in the early 1970s, I never would have believed there were so many different designs. I was first attracted to the bright designs of fruit and flowers and then founded a business making one-of-a-kind clothes. Now, when I search for tablecloths to use in my garments, I am constantly surprised to find new combinations of the fruit and flowers that originally drew my attention.

My most frequently asked question is where do you get all the tablecloths? I work very hard at finding each one that I use. Large antique shows seem to be the best place to find them. There are dealers who specialize in vintage fabric and others who might have only one cloth. When you shop at these type of shows, there is always an awareness that vintage tablecloths are special. I also find them at antique shops or malls as I travel and at the occasional estate sale or thrift shop. Prices vary greatly based on many factors—tablecloth size, desirability of the design, stains, and the type of place you are shopping. There are values with the photo captions in the book. They are not intended to set prices, but do reflect what I consider fair for a tablecloth in great condition found mainly in the Midwest. Remember that prices vary widely between yard sales and antique shows. We all must decide what we can afford to spend for a part of our rich textile history.

My second most often asked question is how do you get out all the old stains? My answer is always the same. I try to buy tablecloths with as few stains as possible! The home chemistry of removing forty- or fifty-year-old spots simply eludes me. Soaking overnight in cool water with Biz™ has been useful in removing the yellowing of age and discolored areas along fold lines. The people I know who are the most successful at removing old stains recommend one of the following two methods: a) spray the stain with a four-to-one solution of bleach and water, or b) cover the stain with fresh lemon juice and salt. Both of these techniques are followed by laying the tablecloth on the grass in the sun. It seems that the sun is a key ingredient. Good luck with the stain removal. I recommend that you practice on tablecloths that have been purchased inexpensively.

Unlike the first book, in this volume, I do not have all the tablecloths with the same design in more than one color together in one chapter. These tablecloths I call double takes and am always pleased to find them. This volume does have it's share of double takes though, see how many you can find. It amazes me how the same design can look so totally different. Happy hunting for double takes and every beautiful tablecloth that you can find.

# *Rose Blooms* 1

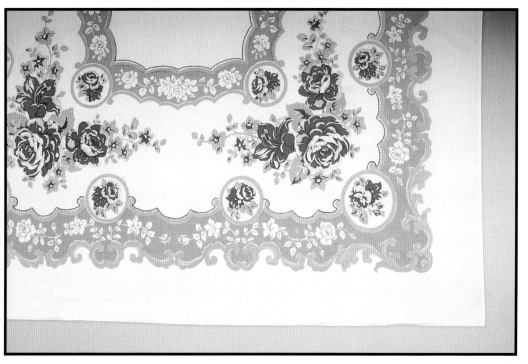

Blue and peach scalloped border with roses in frames and bouquets. $20-40.

Scalloped ribbon creates border for pink roses. $20-40.

Wide yellow bands on cloth highlight bunches of roses. $20-40.

Gray center and border highlight pink roses and rosebuds scattered over center. $20-35.

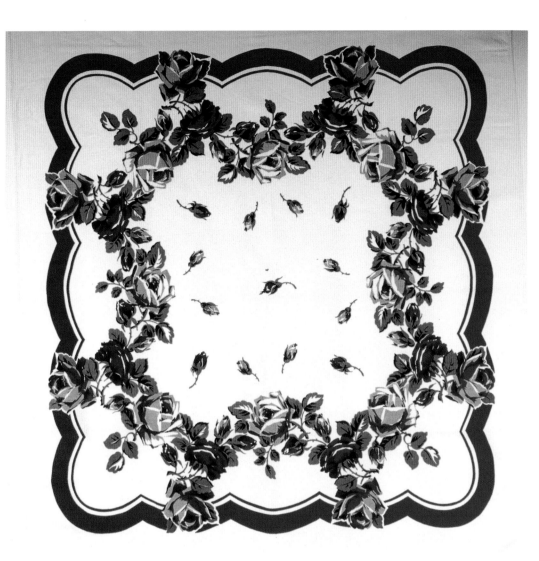

Red scalloped border with intertwining pink and red roses. $20-40.

Large yellow roses create border around cloth. $20-35.

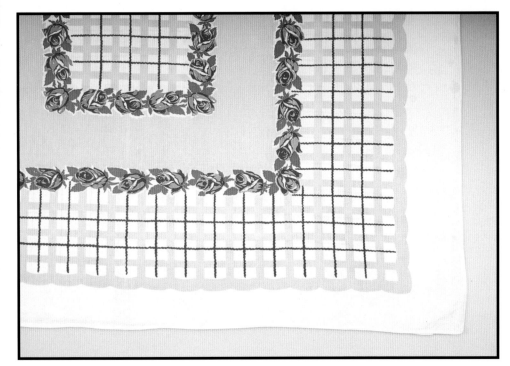

Turquoise and rose plaid at center and border surrounded by two rose borders. $20-35.

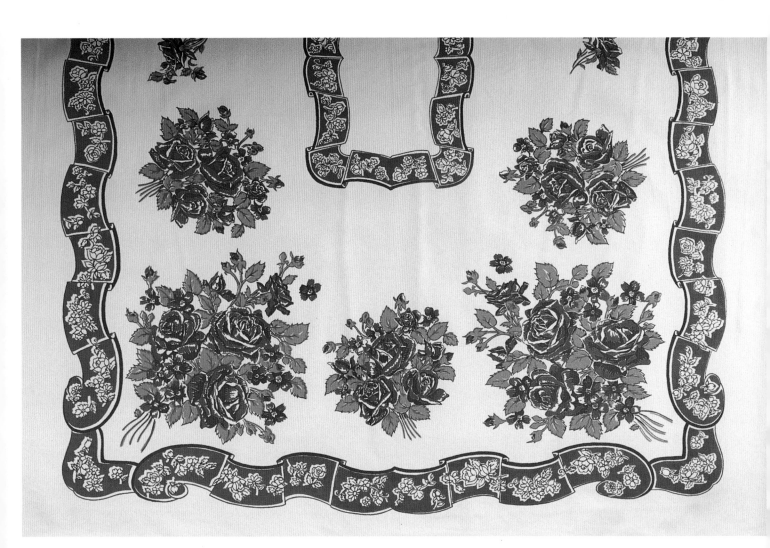

Double blue ribbon borders with bouquets of blue roses. $20-35.

Yellow center and border highlight pink roses. $20-35.

Small bouquets of blue roses spaced evenly over entire cloth. $20-35.

Bouquets of red roses in corners and chain of red roses highlight pink center. $20-25.

Blue roses floating over rows of yellow stripes that diminish in size toward center. $20-35.

Pink roses and buds in allover design. $20-30.

Large white roses connected by ribbons cover cloth. $20-35.

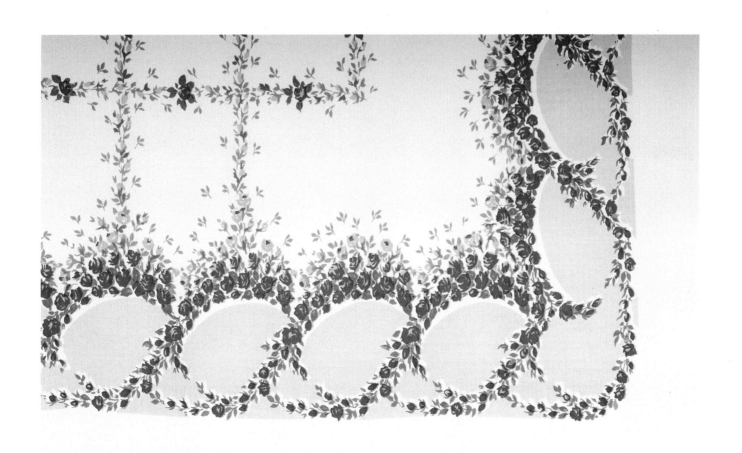

Pink border with loads of red and pink rosebuds. $20-40.

Blue foliage border sets off beautiful red roses. $20-40.

Yellow center and border with large pink roses framing center. $20-35.

Wide red border with interior border of intertwining blue roses. $20-35.

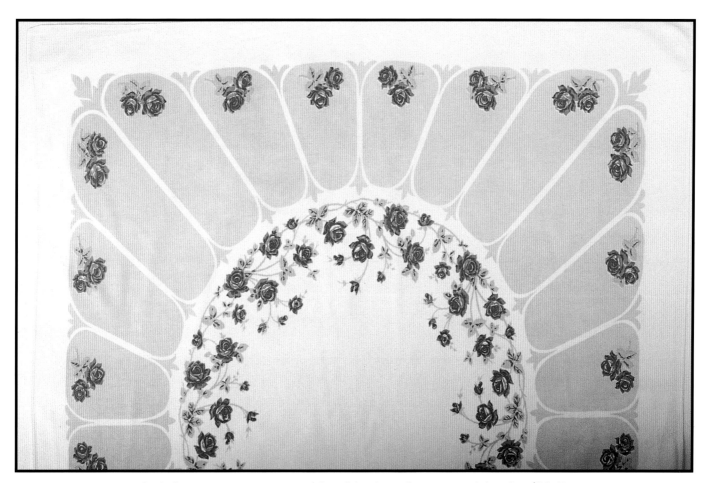

Oval of turquoise roses at center with pink border and roses around the edge. $20-40.

Soft blue border with branches of opening roses. $20-30.

Blue background highlights white roses tied together with ribbon. $20-40.

Green background shows off turquoise roses that circle center and fan out to corners. $20-35.

Red roses and border tied together with burgundy ribbon and bows. $20-35.

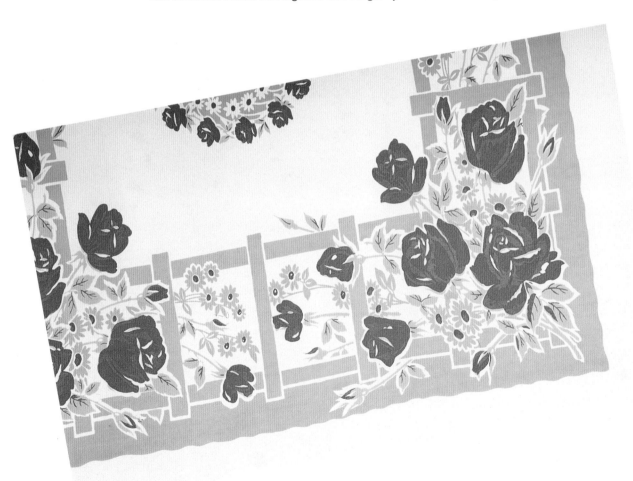

Blue trellis border highlights bouquets of red roses. $20-40.

# Dogwood Blossoms 2

Blue border and center with white blooms around both. $20-35.

Pink background with dogwood over diagonal clusters of polka-dots. $20-35.

Blue border and center with sprays of pink and white dogwood. $20-35.

Pink dogwood on blue border with scattered blooms on blue center. $20-35.

Peach and yellow dogwood borders with scattered blooms on yellow center. $20-35.

Scalloped pink center and border with groups of white dogwood. $20-30.

Teal background and scalloped border with intertwining white dogwood. $20-30.

Red background with groups of dogwood border and blossoms over center. $20-30.

Small bunches of pink dogwood spaced evenly over cloth. $20-30.

Blue checked center and blue border with sprays of yellow dogwood. $20-35.

Teal center surrounded by dogwood with border of leaves. $20-30.

Double red borders overlaid with white dogwood, scattered blooms in center. $20-30.

Pink border and wide central stripe with pink and white blossoms. $20-35.

Crisscrossing rows of red, white, and blue dogwood. $20-35.

# *Terrific Tulips* 3

Striking brown background with white polka-dots showcase large corner groups of pink tulips. $20-40.

Red background with bouquets of
turquoise and green tulips. $20-35.

Lavender tulips grow around the borders of this cloth. $20-30.

Multiple pink tulips bloom around this cloth with interior borders of pink and gray. $20-35.

Burgundy and red floral borders with large corner bunches of tulips. $20-30.

Red background with diagonally placed white tulips. $20-30.

Green and white set off the profusion of yellow tulips. $20-30.

Pink tulips circle cloth between scalloped burgundy borders. $20-35.

Double scalloped seafoam borders showcase huge bouquet of peach tulips. $20-35.

Double scalloped peach borders showcase
huge bouquet of seafoam tulips. $20-35.

Burgundy border and polka-dots with tulips growing around the edges. $20-35.

Red tulips surround interior pink borders. $20-35.

Pink border and center with small blue tulips
in plume shapes. $20-35.

# *Delightful Daisies* 4

Dark red background covered with sprays of white daises. $20-30.

Bright yellow background with white and red daises as the border. $20-30.

Multiple blue borders showcase mounds of yellow daises. $20-30.

Red background with falling leaves and daises. $20-30.

Red and pink plaid background with white daises scattered as the border. $20-30.

Gray border with yellow center show off daises growing toward center. $20-30.

Yellow border with green center show off daises growing toward center. $20-30.

Pink oval border and center with groups of yellow daises. $20-30.

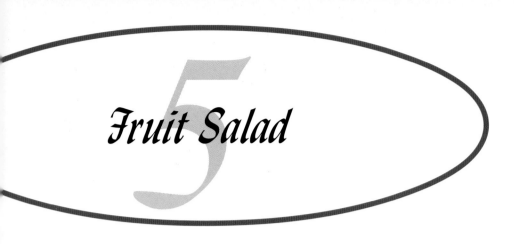

# Fruit Salad

Bright bunches of red cherries spaced evenly over cloth. $20-35.

Red background sets off frames of different fruits. $20-35.

Scalloped peach border with crisscrossed rows of luscious strawberries. $20-35.

Double border of grapes, pears, plums, and apples. $20-35.

Blue squares set off different bunches of fruit. $20-35.

Blue center and ribbon border tie together bunches of fruit. $20-35.

Red and blue scalloped borders highlight bunches of calico fruit. $20-35.

Dark green center highlights border
of pink and red fruit. $20-35.

Individual floral frames showcase groups
of fruit and flowers. $20-35.

Multiple blue borders with red fruit and flowers. $20-35.

Two shades of blue highlight small groups of fruit and flowers. $20-35.

Corner fruit baskets and grapes all over. $20-35.

Red and white checked background with a border of blue and yellow fruit. $20-35.

Swags of colorful fruit held together with burgundy bows. $20-35.

Yellow background shows off corner groups of fruit and scattered berries. $20-35.

Multiple red and yellow borders with baskets of veggies. $20-35.

Orange, yellow, and green border with scattered fruit. $20-35.

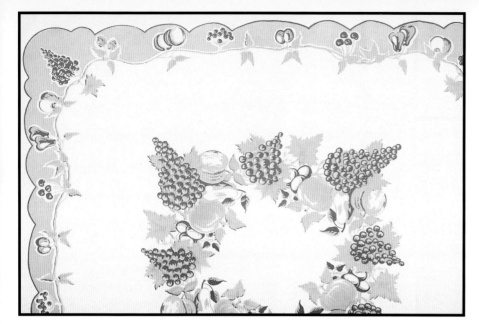

Central and exterior borders of yellow and blue fruit and large bunches of grapes. $20-35.

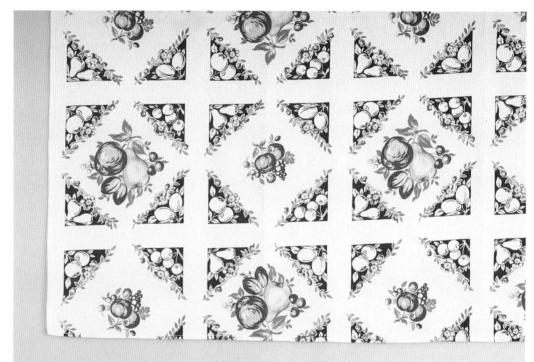

Blue and white corners highlight groups of fruit in quilt-like fashion. $20-35.

Burgundy fruit border with central baskets of fruit and second strawberry border. $20-35.

Evenly spaced baskets of lavender and golden fruit. $20-30.

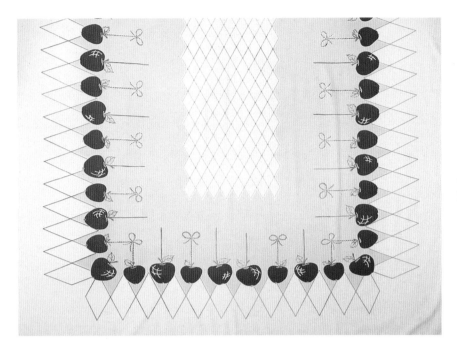

Teal and gold diamond design with border of red apples. $20-30.

Red border with interior fruit and small fruit pieces scattered over center. $20-30.

Green background with large central fruit basket and smaller baskets as border. $20-35.

Double borders of intertwined grapes and leaves. $20-30.

Small bunches of fruit evenly spaced over cloth. $20-30.

Multiple gray borders with swags of fruit cascading toward edges. $20-35.

Small groups of fruit evenly spaced over cloth. $20-30.

Peach center and scrolled frames for border of teal and yellow fruit. $20-35.

Red and green stripes set off golden veggies and leaves. $20-35.

Blue center and border with bunches of grapes. $20-35.

Borders of bows and scallops show off baskets of fruit. $20-35.

Colorful border with central profusion of fruit. $20-35.

Sectioned bunches of fruit and flowers all over cloth. $20-35.

Central burgundy blocks of white fruit with burgundy border and green fruit. $20-35.

Interior border of fruit baskets with yellow exterior border covered with fruit. $20-30.

Fence type border with baskets overflowing with fruit and flowers. $20-35.

Colorful fruit and yellow scalloped border with four large bunches of fruit. $20-35.

Pink and blue borders and fruit. $20-30.

Green border with interior border of fruit and foliage. $20-30.

Bunches of fruit with yellow border and fruit scattered over center. $20-30.

Colorful vertical stripes with horizontal stripes of fruit. $20-35.

Red, blue, and yellow border with baskets of fruit and flowers. $20-35.

Border baskets of veggies in burgundy, green, and gold. $20-35.

Mounds of veggies on all sides and veggies scattered over center. $20-35.

Veggies around burgundy border and peas scattered over center. $20-35.

Border baskets of veggies and veggies scattered over center. $20-35.

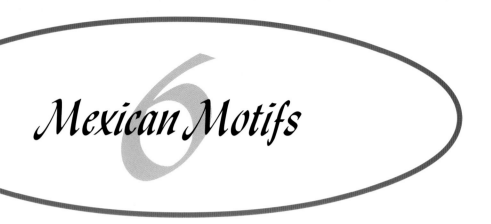

# *Mexican Motifs* 6

Clay pot border with palm trees growing toward center. Corner scenes of Mexican life. $20-35.

Mexican blanket stripes frame southwestern imagery. $20-40.

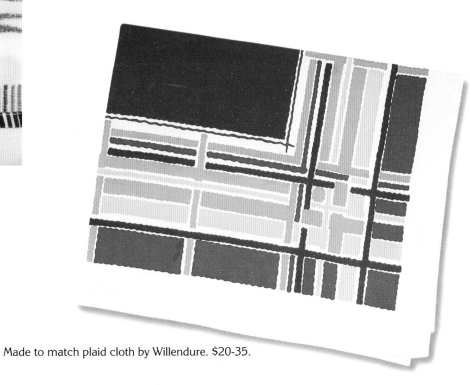

Willendure label of previous cloth.

Made to match plaid cloth by Willendure. $20-35.

Multiple striped borders with the widest showing Mexican figures. $20-35.

Blue and yellow borders highlight palms and scenes of daily living. $20-35.

Picture frame border with scenes of pots, cactus, fruit, and sombreros.
Second striped blanket border and images over entire cloth. $20-35.

Colorful pottery borders with different scenes over entire cloth. $20-35.

Scenes of sombreros, people, fruit, and pottery spaced over entire cloth. $20-35.

Gold and black border of kitchen utensils with salt and pepper shakers all over center. $20-35.

Same cloth in pink.

Gray and gold border with center covered in calico kitchen utensils and flowers. $20-30.

Multiple borders frame scenes of household items. $20-30.

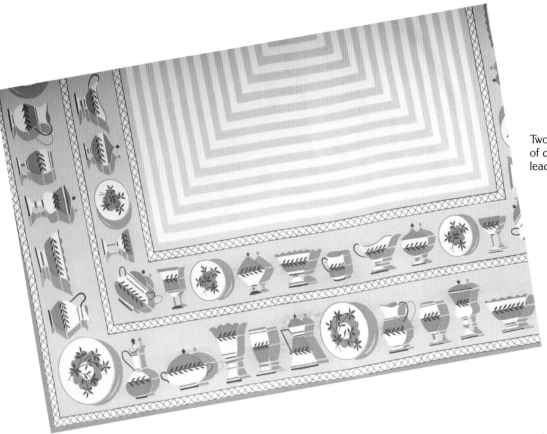

Two pink and turquoise borders of dinnerware with many stripes leading to center. $20-30.

Teal background with border frames showing plates and other household items. $20-30.

Chartreuse center with border scenes of farm and kitchen goodies. $20-35.

Turquoise background with frames showing jugs and urns around border. $20-30.

Two borders of fancy spice jugs and flowers on this gray and chartreuse cloth. $20-30.

# Ivy & Foliage 8

Colorful border of red, green, and yellow foliage. $20-30.

Two tone blue borders and allover design of ferns. $20-35.

Green border with foliage of subtle color. $15-25.

Multiple borders of ivy. $15-25.

Two borders of tan leaves on soft green background. $15-25.

Pink border and center showing tan ivy. $15-25.

Dark green cloth using negative space to create ivy design. $15-25.

Chartreuse cloth using negative space to create intertwining foliage design. $15-25.

# Specialty Cloths

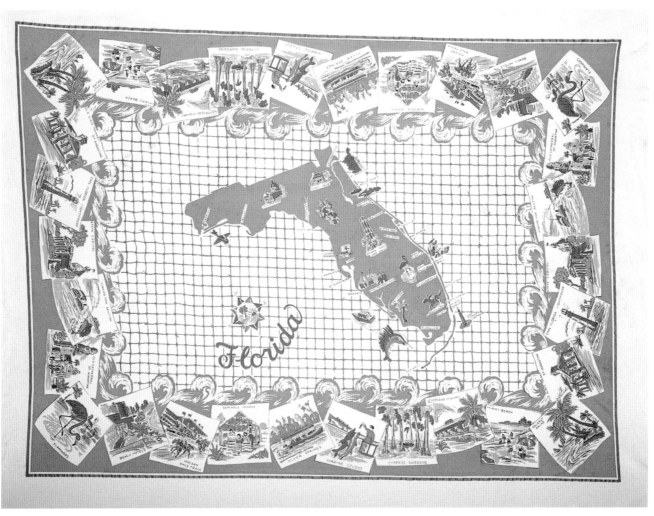

Large gold map of Florida with points of interest around border. $35-85.

Florida banner, palm trees, and Florida scenes around border. $25-50.

Green Florida map with points of interest around border. $35-75.

Flower of the month cloth in bright colors. $25-40.

Border of cherry blossoms and scenes from Washington, D.C. $25-50.

Corners of hula girls and palm trees. $25-50.

Border of geraniums and gardening goodies. $20-35.

Green background using negative space to create clothes pins. $20-35.

The farmer and his wife. Note the faces on the veggies. $25-40.

Border with stagecoach and western life. $25-40.

Look before you eat! Great calorie border. $25-45.

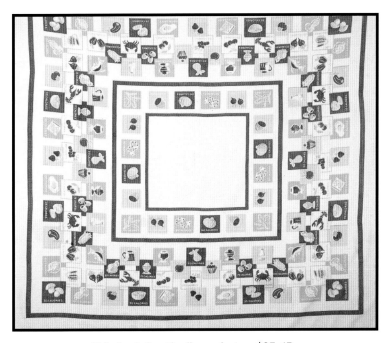

Calorie cloth with allover design. $25-45.

Chicken today. Feathers tomorrow. $25-40.

Border of framed chicken and roosters. $23-35.

Red and black rooster and farmyard border. $25-35.

Red and blue bird of paradise. $25-35.

Pastel chicken and rooster borders. $25-35.

# *Pennsylvania Dutch Influence*

*10*

Scalloped borders of red and blue with tulips,
windmills, and Dutch people. $20-35.

Squares of color with Pennsylvania
Dutch designs. $20-30.

Red center and border separated by Pennsylvania Dutch scenes. $20-30.

Pink and yellow squares with scenes and sayings. $20-30.

Squares with stylized tulips in red, blue, and yellow. $20-30.

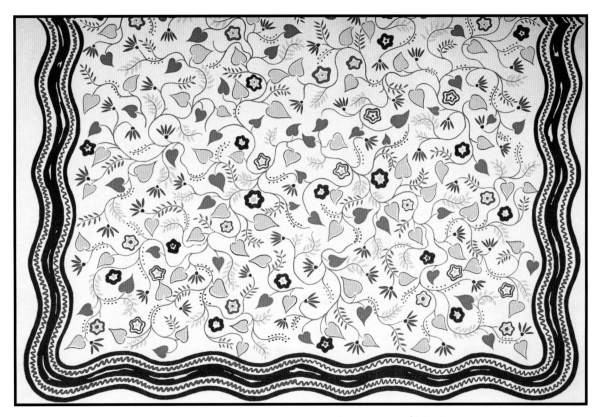

Wavy red borders with allover Dutch floral designs. $20-30.

Border of framed Dutch boys and girls with tulips. $20-30.

Traditional Dutch motifs as borders in red and ivory. $20-30.

# *Garden of Flowers* 11

Center circle of turquoise lilacs with lilac blooms all over. $20-35.

Double borders of yellow with red and ivory flowers. $20-35.

Exterior ribbon border. Interior border of pink and red flowers tied with bows. $20-35.

Bright pink border with profusion of pink and blue flowers and leaves. $20-35.

Intertwining pink and gray flowers surround center and edge. $20-35.

Pink border with bouquets of pink and yellow blossoms. $20-35.

Blue background with white blossoms held together by white ribbon. $20-35.

Gray border surrounded by lilacs and blooms scattered over center. $20-35.

Turquoise and orange sections and borders with corner bouquets. $20-30.

Chartreuse checked center and border with tassels. Corner bouquets and floating flowers. $20-30.

Corner bouquets with iris. Border accented with ferns. $20-35.

Red and gray flowers flowing over cloth inside gray border. $20-30.

Curving blue border with rows of blooms. Vase of red and blue flowers in corner. $20-35.

Many rows of blue and green flowers leading to center. $20-35.

Pink and red borders covered with white and gray blooms. $20-30.

Pink scalloped borders and ribbon holding together blue carnations. $20-35.

Purple and lavender gladiolas create border for this cloth. $20-30.

Red and yellow blooms travel with a graceful pattern of leaves over this cloth. $20-35.

Pink and red petunias circle
the edge of this cloth. $20-30.

Three rows of small flowers separated by rows
of ribbon and bows create the border. $20-30.

Blue border with corner bouquets. Ribbons separate flower clusters in center. $20-35.

Blue center with bows and flowers lead to gray border. $20-35.

Blue bouquets inside multiple green scalloped borders. $20-35.

Two pink borders separated by rows of small flowers.
Single blossoms scattered over center. $20-35.

Chartreuse center with pink frame border showing
floral clusters. $20-30.

Pretty yellow and red clusters cover center. Smaller groups toward border. $20-35.

*Opposite page:* Groups of small red blooms
alternate with gray in allover pattern. $20-35.

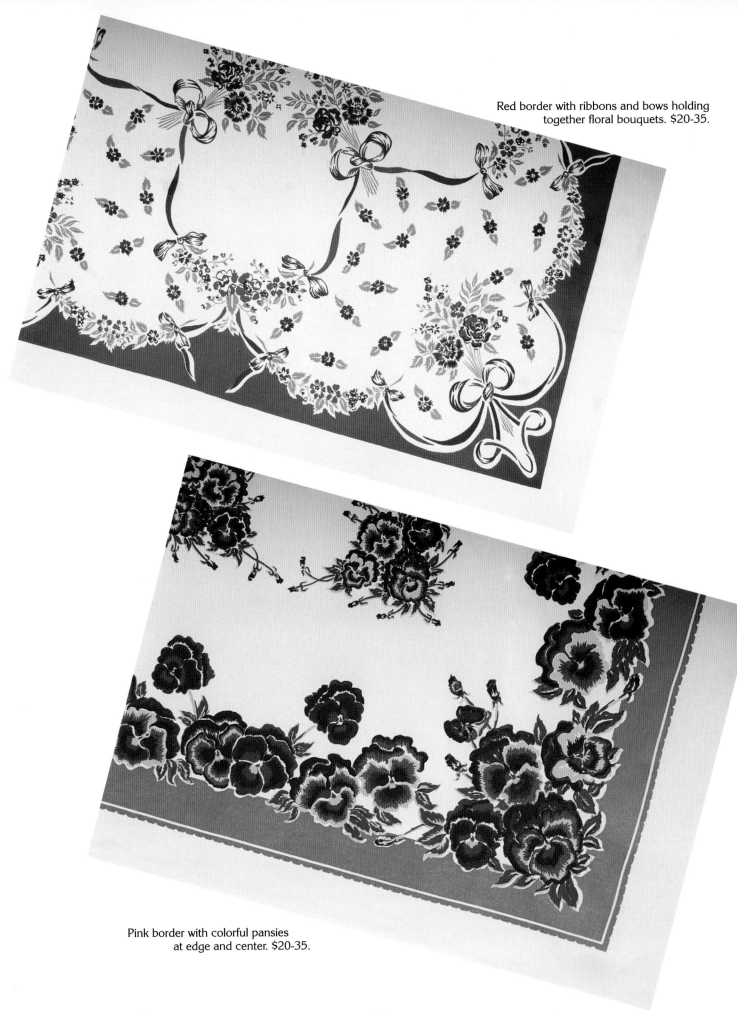

Red border with ribbons and bows holding
together floral bouquets. $20-35.

Pink border with colorful pansies
at edge and center. $20-35.

Gray and white borders for pink scattered blooms. $20-30.

Soft green border with stylized blooms of lavender and pink. $20-30.

Border of large blue blossoms surround this cloth. $20-35.

Two rows of pink and blue blooms inside blue striped border. $20-35.

Soft green background with rows of white flowers creating the border. $20-30.

Soft peach and gray create this delicate floral design. $20-30.

Multiple pink borders and center create space for gray and burgundy blossoms. $20-30.

Red center shows
off border of large
brown-eyed susans.
$20-35.

Graceful red and gray design at corners and smaller red floral border at center. $20-30.

Navy border shows off pink floral border going toward central blue area with blossoms. $20-35.

Border of flowers and green lattice to green center with corner blossoms. $20-35.

Yellow border and central area. Large pink bouquets in corners and pink blooms around center. $20-35.

Small red blossoms all over cloth. $20-35.

Lavender corners highlight
large floral bouquets. $20-35.

Pink ribbon flows around edge covered
by pretty blossoms and foliage. $20-35.

Blue rectangular areas show off blooms of red and white. $20-30.

Graceful swags hold together bouquets all around cloth. $20-35.

Yellow background show large corner groups of forsythia. $20-30.

Soft blue background with large bouquets in corners. $20-35.

Yellow fence background shows off large red and yellow blooms. $20-35.

Gray and white center and border create space for bunches of pink blooms. $20-30.

Red and white squares show off floral groups around the edge of this cloth. $20-30.

Red ribbon border contains field of red and lavender blossoms. $20-35.

Borders of pink and blue stripes alternate with rows of small flowers. $20-35.

Bright blossoms of red, yellow, and blue all around. $20-35.

Seafoam lattice and border create space for pink and white blooms. $20-35.

Large turquoise blossoms with burgundy leaves all over cloth. $20-35.

Blue border sets off two rows of red and blue flowers. $20-35.

Gray feathered and sectioned border frame groups of yellow blooms. $20-30.

Large golden flowers wind their way over green borders. $20-35.

Large pink blossoms over blue background with
white leaf center using the negative space. $20-35.

Pink plaid creates sections for small golden bouquets. $20-30.

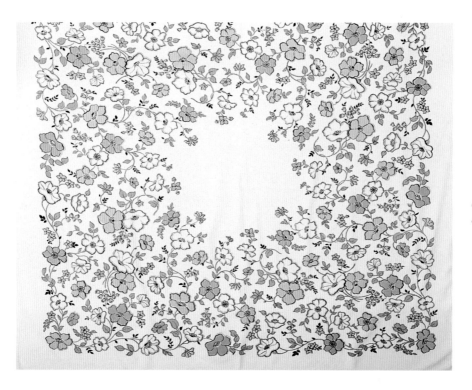

Cloth covered by pink, gray, and white blooms. $20-30.

Soft blue border and center surrounded by rows of red flowers. $20-35.

Red floral groups in frames at center and around cloth edge. $20-35.

Pink background shows off white design created from the negative space. $20-30.

Bright bouquets at angles create squares all over cloth. $20-35.

Stylized blossoms in squares with
multiple colorful borders. $20-35.

Multiple borders alternating pink and royal blue blossoms. $20-35.

Red an ivory zigzag border with large blossoms and small blossoms in center. $20-35.

Blue and burgundy borders with bouquets of the same colors. $20-30.

Red borders, ribbons, and bows holding bunches of pink clover. $20-35.

Red and white striped border highlights subtle gray blossoms. $20-30.

Burgundy borders with stylized blue and green flowers. $20-30.

Multi-colored scalloped borders with large corner bouquets and blue center. $20-35.

Chartreuse plaid background shows off fruit and flowers in red and yellow. $20-35.

Multiple navy and red borders with dots and flowers. $20-35.

Red ribbon border with bouquets leading to center. $20-30.

Yellow diamonds highlight bouquets of pink. $20-35.

Red center and border surrounded by small yellow blossoms. $20-30.

Red ribbons intertwine holding small bouquets. $20-30.

Rows of pastel blossoms intersect at corners of moss green border surrounded by ribbon. $20-35.

Border of small leaves on pink and white background. $20-30.

Blue ribbons and bows intersect over cloth holding bouquets of red. $20-35.

Cloth covered with pink and blue blossoms and multiple pink borders. $20-35.

Bouquets of yellow daffodils evenly spaced over cloth. $20-35.

Pink blooms on soft yellow squares that alternate with white. $20-35.

Green and white squares with pink blooms cascading around the border. $20-35.

Soft orange fruit and flower border. $20-30.

Blue bouquets held together by swirls of leaves. $20-35.

Beautiful peach border shows off large central spray of lavender and peach. $20-35.

Two tone green shows off groups of pink
and yellow blooms. $20-35.

Yellow background with white scalloped border
for blooms of pink and white. $20-30.

Small central lavender blossoms and large bouquets in corners. $20-30.

Fancy lavender border and baskets hold blooms. $20-35.

Red background with corner displays of chartreuse and white blossoms. $20-35.

Soft blue background with border of pink blooms and daises over center. $20-35.

Red blooms drape over red striped border. $20-30.

Diagonal lavender stripes with double border of red flowers. $20-35.

Center of turquoise intertwining buds with turquoise border and pink buds. $20-35.

Great blue and purple borders lead to center of red and purple flowers. $20-35.

Bright border of red and peach intertwining blossoms. $20-30.

Turquoise background shows off border or springtime blooms. $20-35.

Blue and lavender borders with flowing design of pink blossoms. $20-35.

Soft green border with ribbon holds garland of pink and yellow. $20-35.

Turquoise border and central checks with colorful flowers. $20-35.

Simple design of blue and white with garland inside border. $20-30.

Red and white with flowers in stencil-like design. $20-30.

Primary colors with lovely calico flowers. $20-35.

Red and green borders and large
bouquets pointing at center. $20-35.

Yellow border and center
with pink and yellow blooms
between. $20-35.

Simple design of red and gray
bouquets and borders. $20-30.

Multiple pink and green borders with bouquets of large lilies. $20-30.

Triangles filled with green and gold blooms create border design. $20-30.

Pink center and striped border show pastel corner bouquets. $20-35.

Single large blooms repeat, evenly spaced over cloth. $20-30.

Bulbs sprout toward edges and center on this simple cloth. $20-30.

Wavy red border with ribbons and bows show off large turquoise blooms. $20-35.

Pink border covered with small turquoise bouquets. $20-30.

Double borders of red, white, and burgundy blossoms. $20-30.

Double rows of sunflowers circle this cloth with pink outside border. $20-35.

Red and orange blossoms at center in circle and at cloth border with red outside border. $20-30.

Evenly spaced groups of reddish, pink daffodils cover this beige background. $20-30.

Scattered pink and yellow blossoms over center with garland covering blue border. $20-35.

Pink ribbon tied bouquets evenly spaced over cloth. $20-35.

*Opposite page:* Red borders separate groups of blooms in this allover primary color design. $20-35.

Multiple borders of pastel fruit and flowers. $20-30.

Dark blue lattice separates groups of red blossoms. $20-35.

Border of white daises on navy background with central bouquets of red. $20-35.

Stylized blossoms of red and navy create multiple borders. $20-30.

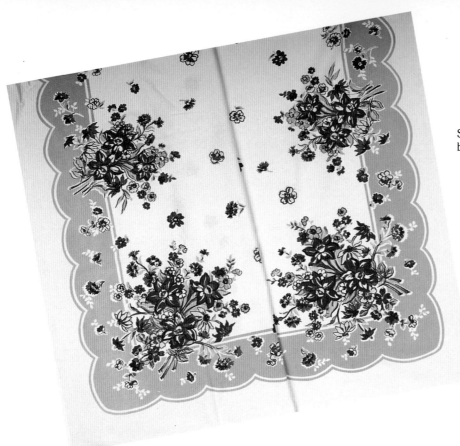

Scalloped pastel blue border highlights bright bouquets and scattered blooms. $20-35.

Bouquets of pink and blue gracefully flow to yellow border. $20-35.

Small blue and red bouquets between blue scalloped borders. $20-35.

Burgundy border covered by pink and green garland. $20-30.

Beautiful blue border shows off large central spray of pink, red, and blue flowers. $20-35.

Pretty border of yellow blossoms and pink fruit. $20-35.

Evenly spaced groups of red hibiscus. $20-35.

Evenly spaced groups of golden hibiscus. $20-35.

Peach central area with large corner bouquets of green hibiscus. $20-30.

Colorful border of ferns with yellow and orange hibiscus. $20-35.

Pretty yellow border with red blooms and bouquets. $20-30.

Yellow and two shades of pink create pretty central bouquets and border. $20-35.

Peach and green geometric shapes overlaid with large blossoms. $20-35.

Pink center with burgundy border
showcase large bouquets. $20-35.

Yellow background with green border
highlight colorful blossoms and
scattered daises. $20-35.

Red and burgundy bulbs sprout from burgundy border. $20-30.

Blue and white blooms with yellow leaves surround border of burgundy cloth. $20-35.

Pink oval frames and border surround blue blossoms. $20-35.

Turquoise and white center and border create space for pink and blue garland. $20-30.

Evenly spaced large yellow blooms surround cloth. $20-35.

Alternating rust and white spaces filled with flowers. $20-35.

Interior border with bouquets of flowers and exterior lattice border. $20-35.

Blue border with large bouquets of pink daffodils. $20-35.

Borders of gray and white tassels with pink ribbon hold bouquets of pink blooms. $20-35.

Blooms tied together with ribbon march around border.
Corner bouquets and central spray of chartreuse and red. $20-35.

Peach flower and ribbon border with bouquets of turquoise violets. $20-35.

Evenly spaced pink, yellow, and blue clusters with scattered blue blooms. $20-35.

Yellow border with floral garland highlight bouquets of red and yellow flowers with sprigs of blue. $20-35.

Multiple borders of blue and small blooms. $20-30.

Crosses of red and blue evenly spaced over gray and white background. $20-35.